Date: 10/7/21

J BIO RAPINOE
Fishman, Jon M.,
Megan Rapinoe /

Lerner SPORTS

SPORTS
ALL-ST★RS

MEGAN
RAPINOE

Jon M. Fishman

Lerner Publications ◆ Minneapolis

Lerner Publications Company
An imprint of Lerner Publishing Group, Inc.
241 First Avenue North
Minneapolis, MN 55401 USA

For reading levels and more information, look up this title at www.lernerbooks.com.

Main body text set in Albany Std 15/22. Typeface provided by Agfa.

Editor: Shee Yang

Library of Congress Cataloging-in-Publication Data

Names: Fishman, Jon M., author.
Title: Megan Rapinoe / Jon M. Fishman.
Description: Minneapolis : Lerner Publications, 2021. | Series: Sports all-stars (lerner sports) | Includes bibliographical references and index. | Audience: Ages 7–11 | Audience: Grades K–1 | Summary: "World league soccer player Megan Rapinoe has wowed on the international stage multiple times. Beyond having a long list of accolades, Rapinoe's passion for sports, love, and people is what sets her apart. Learn more about this exciting athlete and her journey to the top"— Provided by publisher.
Identifiers: LCCN 2019041624 (print) | LCCN 2019041625 (ebook) | ISBN 9781541598959 (library binding) | ISBN 9781728401034 (ebook)
Subjects: LCSH: Rapinoe, Megan—Juvenile literature. | Women soccer players—United States—Biography—Juvenile literature. | Soccer players—United States—Biography—Juvenile literature.
Classification: LCC GV942.7.R366 F57 2020 (print) | LCC GV942.7.R366 (ebook) | DDC 796.334092 [B]—dc23

LC record available at https://lccn.loc.gov/2019041624
LC ebook record available at https://lccn.loc.gov/2019041625

Manufactured in the United States of America
1-48084-48744-3/5/2020

CONTENTS

COCAPTAIN AMERICA

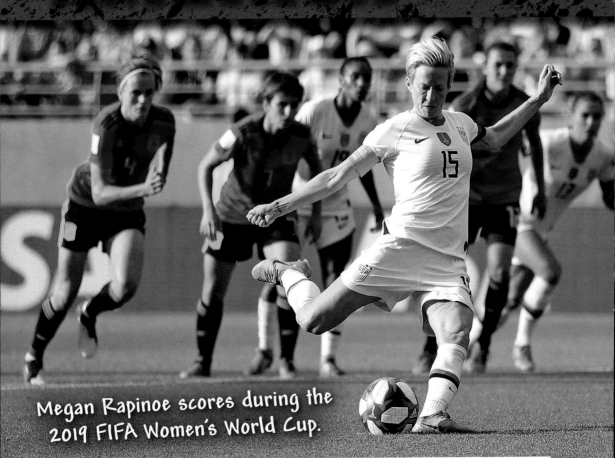

Megan Rapinoe scores during the 2019 FIFA Women's World Cup.

The world watched as Megan Rapinoe stood alone on the soccer field. Players from the United States Women's National Team (USWNT) and Spain's national team stood behind her. Fans in the stadium and millions more around the globe followed every move as Rapinoe stepped forward and blasted the ball.

- **Date of birth:** July 5, 1985

- **Position:** forward

- **League:** National Women's Soccer League (NWSL)

- **Professional highlights:** has played for teams in France and Australia; helped the United States win the Women's World Cup in 2015 and 2019; won the Golden Boot Award at the 2019 Women's World Cup

- **Personal highlights:** has a twin sister named Rachael Rapinoe; played soccer at the University of Portland; runs a business with her sister called Rapinoe SC

Rapinoe and the USWNT were playing Spain in the Women's World Cup on June 24, 2019. The winner would advance to the **quarterfinal** round of the tournament. Rapinoe's **penalty kick** streaked just above the grass. The goalie dove in the wrong direction as the ball sailed into the net. Goal! The USWNT took a 1–0 lead.

Rapinoe celebrates with her teammates after making her first goal during the 2019 FIFA Women's World Cup.

Rapinoe was one of three USWNT cocaptains at the 2019 Women's World Cup. The other two cocaptains were Alex Morgan and Carli Lloyd.

Rapinoe's teammates hugged her. The USWNT hadn't allowed a goal against them in more than 600 minutes of game time. It was a streak that stretched back to April. With a one-goal lead, the team felt confident they could win.

Spain fought back hard. Less than three minutes after Rapinoe's goal, they attacked. Spain's Lucia Garcia passed to Jennifer Hermoso. With the US goalie out of position, Hermoso shot. The ball zipped into the net to tie the game 1–1.

Rapinoe and her teammates were stunned by Spain's goal. But the USWNT recovered quickly. The teams battled for the next goal. The United States took shot after shot, but they couldn't get the ball past Spain's goalie.

With about 15 minutes left in the second half, everything changed. One of Spain's defenders took down the US's Rose Lavelle near Spain's goal. The referee called a **foul** on the play. That meant a penalty kick for the USWNT. Once again, the team chose Rapinoe to take the kick. She scored with another low shot.

The USWNT held on for a 2–1 win. To Rapinoe, it seemed as if each game in the tournament was tougher than the one before. After beating Spain, she had one message for her team: "Keep grinding, keep together."

Rapinoe (*front*) and cocaptain Alex Morgan celebrate after a US goal.

Redding, California

Megan Rapinoe was born on July 5, 1985—11 minutes later than her twin sister, Rachael. The sisters were the youngest of six siblings. They grew up together in a **rural** area near Redding, California.

Megan and Rachael loved to play outside. They fished for crayfish in the creek. They played with the family's cats and dogs and climbed a giant oak tree. They especially enjoyed playing soccer together. It was one of many sports the sisters enjoyed. They played football, baseball, and basketball too.

German forward Simone Laudehr (*left*) and Megan fight for the ball during the first half of the FIFA Under-19 Women's World Championship semifinal in Bangkok on November 24, 2004.

In 2002, Megan began playing soccer for the Elk Grove Pride in Elk Grove, California. She played for Elk Grove to compete against better teams than her high school team faced. But it took more than two hours to reach Elk Grove by car. So Megan sometimes skipped practices to stay home and play soccer with her sister.

Playing with Rachael allowed Megan to come up with her own moves and ideas about how to play. "I was never told what I should be doing, I just played how I played," she said. Her Elk Grove coaches gave her the freedom to be creative too.

After high school, the sisters attended the University of Portland in Oregon. They played on the school's soccer team. Megan scored 15 goals and 13 **assists** in 25 games in 2005.

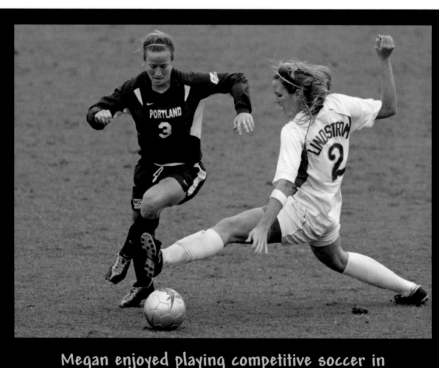

Megan enjoyed playing competitive soccer in college. It earned her the National Freshman of the Year award from the *Soccer Times*.

A standout athlete, Megan (*center*) enjoyed celebrating goals with her Portland Pilot teammates.

In 2006, Megan began training with the USWNT in addition to playing for Portland. But on October 5, she hurt her knee and missed the rest of the season. The next year, she played just two games before another knee injury ended her season.

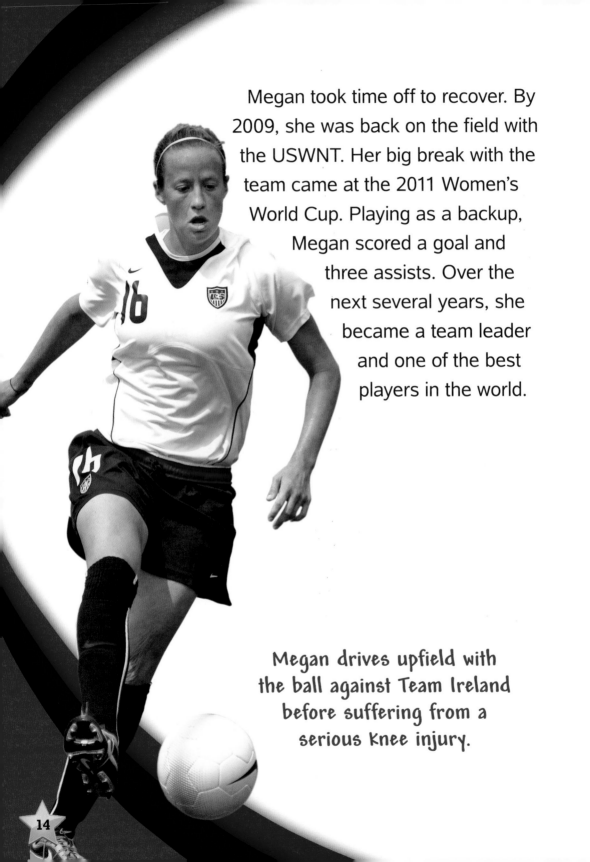

Megan took time off to recover. By 2009, she was back on the field with the USWNT. Her big break with the team came at the 2011 Women's World Cup. Playing as a backup, Megan scored a goal and three assists. Over the next several years, she became a team leader and one of the best players in the world.

Megan drives upfield with the ball against Team Ireland before suffering from a serious knee injury.

Rapinoe's outgoing and assertive personality made her a natural leader for her team.

During a 90-minute soccer match, Rapinoe runs constantly. When the USWNT has the ball, she never stops attacking and trying to score. When the other team has it, she supports her teammates on defense. To play with as much energy in the 90th minute as she does in the first minute, she makes sure her body is in the best shape possible.

Rapinoe says **weight training** helps her play her best. Lifting heavy weights in a gym makes all of her muscles stronger. During games, her muscles take longer to tire out.

Rapinoe's history of knee injuries influences her workouts. She often exercises with stretchy bands that cause less stress to her knees than heavy weights do. With one band around her knees and another around her ankles, Rapinoe walks, rotates her legs, and squats.

Rapinoe makes sure to train her legs as hard as she trains her upper body. Being strong and healthy keeps her performing at her peak.

Rapinoe stretches often, especially before games, to prevent straining and injuries.

During the soccer season, Rapinoe has practices and games most days. But in the **off-season**, she's on her own for workouts. To make sure she doesn't slack off, she works out every morning. "I try to get up, stick to a plan, work out at the same time every day," she said. "That gets me in the routine and then by midday I'm done."

Rapinoe alternates her kicking leg while keeping the ball in the air. This helps her with control and endurance.

Workouts, games, and practices are exhausting, even for world-class athletes. Rapinoe makes sure to get plenty of downtime to allow her muscles to heal. "I feel like recovery is more important than all of the training that you do," she said.

According to Rapinoe, the most important part of recovery is getting enough sleep. She tries to be asleep by 11:00 each night. She follows that schedule during the season and off-season.

Eating healthful food is another way Rapinoe recovers. After every game, she drinks a **protein** smoothie. The smoothies usually include strawberries, orange juice, almond milk, and protein powder. The protein helps her muscles recover quickly. For meals, she prefers lean meat such as chicken and fish. She eats eggs, grain, and vegetables, especially sweet potatoes.

Rapinoe often takes a three-week vacation during soccer's off-season in November and December. That's the only time of year when she doesn't work out every day.

Rapinoe often interacts with her fans. She offers waves, hugs, and sometimes even takes selfies!

On the field, Rapinoe is full of energy. Her style and vision create chances for her teammates to shine. She's not afraid to tell players and referees exactly what she thinks. Off the field, she lives the same way.

Rapinoe is passionate about helping children, especially young girls who may struggle with finding guidance.

By 2011, Rapinoe's friends and family had known she was gay for years. But after starring in the World Cup that year, she decided to talk publicly about her sexuality. Kids around the world had few famous gay athletes to look up to. She wanted to change that. Rapinoe works hard to promote equal rights for LGBTQIA+ people. She wants to be sure everyone can play sports, no matter their sexual or gender identities.

In August 2016, National Football League quarterback Colin Kaepernick began kneeling as the US national anthem played before games. He said that people

Rapinoe is the first professional white athlete to kneel in support of Colin Kaepernick during the national anthem.

of color were not treated fairly in the United States. By kneeling, Kaepernick was bringing attention to the unfair treatment of people of color.

Other athletes soon followed Kaepernick. Before a soccer match in September, Rapinoe knelt during the anthem. She recognized that she had not experienced racial injustice herself. "But I cannot stand idly by while there are people in this country who have had to deal with that kind of heartache," she said. She later began to stand for the anthem again but refused to sing or place her hand over her heart.

Rapinoe SC

Megan and Rachael Rapinoe run a business called Rapinoe SC. They sell T-shirts, shoes, and other clothing and gear designed and inspired by the sisters. They create clothing for people of all ages and backgrounds.

Rapinoe SC also runs youth training camps for soccer players and teams across the US. Megan says working with kids is her favorite part of the job.

Rapinoe celebrates with her family following a 2019 FIFA Women's World Cup match.

Rapinoe played for the Red Stars for two years.

The Chicago Red Stars were a team in the Women's Professional Soccer (WPS) league. In 2009, Chicago chose Rapinoe with the second overall pick in the league **draft**. But the WPS lasted just two years.

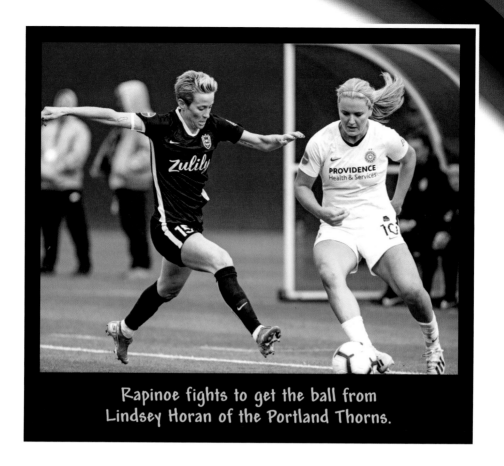

Rapinoe fights to get the ball from
Lindsey Horan of the Portland Thorns.

Rapinoe played for pro teams in Sydney, Australia, and Lyon, France. In 2016, she began playing in Seattle, Washington, for Reign FC of the National Women's Soccer League. But she is most famous for her time with the USWNT.

The United States lost to Japan at the 2011 Women's World Cup. But Rapinoe and the USWNT captured the title in 2015. In 2019, the United States faced France in the World Cup quarterfinal. It was a tough match against the host country's team.

Rapinoe helped Team USA win gold at the 2012 Olympic Games in London, England. She played for the United States again at the 2016 Olympics, but the team finished in fifth place.

Less than five minutes into the game, Rapinoe smashed a shot. France's goalie couldn't see the ball. Goal!

The USWNT held their 1–0 lead in the second half. Teammate Alex Morgan sent a perfect pass to Tobin Heath. Heath raced toward the goal. At the last moment, Heath passed the ball. At first, it looked like a bad pass. But then Rapinoe raced in to blast the ball into the goal. The USWNT won the game 2–1.

The United States beat England and then the Netherlands to win the world title. Rapinoe won the Golden Boot Award as the tournament's top scorer. She hopes to play in the 2020 Summer Olympics, and she'll keep speaking out on important issues. Some people think she should run for political office, even for president of the United States. "I think I'm ready for that next thing," she said.

Rapinoe poses with her trophies after the 2019 Women's World Cup.

All-Star Stats

Some players score a lot of goals, and some players rack up assists. Rapinoe does both. Take a look at where she ranked on the USWNT in total goals and assists in 2019.

Player	Goals	Assists	Total goals and assists
Carli Lloyd	16	5	21
Christen Press	5	12	17
Megan Rapinoe	9	7	16
Lindsey Horan	5	4	9
Alex Morgan	9	3	12
Tobin Heath	7	5	12
Samantha Mewis	6	4	10
Mallory Pugh	6	2	8
Rose Lavelle	4	4	8

Source Notes

8   Steven Goff, "'Winning by Any Means Possible,'
    U.S. Grinds Past Spain to World Cup Quarterfinals,"
    Washington Post, June 24, 2019, https://www.
    washingtonpost.com/sports/2019/06/24/uswnt-spain-
    world-cup/.

12 Gwendolyn Oxenham, "Made of Awesome," *Eight by
    Eight*, April 15, 2015, https://8by8mag.com/megan-
    rapinoe/.

17 Brittney McNamara, "A Day at the Gym with U.S. Soccer
    Stars Megan Rapinoe and Crystal Dunn," *Teen Vogue*,
    June 13, 2019, https://www.teenvogue.com/story/day-
    at-the-gym-us-soccer-megan-rapinoe-crystal-dunn-the-
    hustle.

19 Alyssa Sparacino, "Megan Rapinoe on Why Recovery
    Is Even More Important than Training," *Shape*, July 22,
    2019, https://www.shape.com/celebrities/news/megan-
    rapinoe-recovery-more-important-than-training.

22 "Megan Rapinoe: A Profile of the US Women's
    Co-Captain," BBC News, June 27, 2019, https://www.bbc.
    com/news/newsbeat-48784765.

27 Claire Landsbaum, "Mayor Rapinoe? Senator Rapinoe?
    President Rapinoe?!? In America's World Cup Heroine, a
    Political Star Is Born," *Vanity Fair,* July 15, 2019, https://
    www.vanityfair.com/news/2019/07/megan-rapinoe-
    americas-world-cup-heroine-a-political-star-is-born.

assists: passes that lead to goals

draft: an event in which teams select new players

foul: an instance of breaking the rules of soccer

off-season: the part of the year when a sports league is inactive

penalty kick: a free kick at the goal from 36 feet (11 m) away, awarded by the referee after a foul near the goal

protein: a natural substance that includes ingredients essential for life

quarterfinal: the round of matches before the semifinals of a tournament. Quarterfinal winners must win one more match to reach the finals.

rural: relating to the country or country life

weight training: a system of exercise involving lifting weights to improve strength and endurance

Further Information

Hewson, Anthony K. *Alex Morgan*. Minneapolis: Lerner Publications, 2020.

Hewson, Anthony K. *Megan Rapinoe: Soccer Superstar*. Mankato, MN: Press Room Editions, 2020.

Killion, Ann. *Champions of Women's Soccer*. New York: Philomel Books, 2018.

Rapinoe SC
https://www.rapinoe.us/about/

USWNT
https://www.ussoccer.com/teams/uswnt

Index

Photo Acknowledgments

Image credits: Marc Atkins/Getty Images, pp. 4, 5; Pier Marco Tacca/Getty Images, p. 6; Jean Catuffe/Getty Images, p. 9; Norbert Figueroa/EyeEm/Getty Images, p. 10; Saeed Khan/AFP/Getty Images, p. 11; Rodolfo Gonzalez/NCAA Photos/Getty Images, p. 12; Darren Abate/Getty Images, p. 13; Christian Petersen/Getty Images, p. 14; Ira L. Black/Corbis/Getty Images, p. 15; Elsa/Getty Images, p. 16; Franck Fife/AFP/Getty Images, p. 17; Jewel Samad/AFP/Getty Images, p. 18; Raymond Hall/GC Images/Getty Images, p. 20; Mike Coppola/Getty Images, p. 21; Jamie Sabau/Getty Images, p. 22; Matthew Lewis/FIFA/Getty Images, p. 23; Robin Alam/Icon SMI/Icon Sport Media/Getty Images, p. 24; Lindsey Wasson/Getty Images, p. 25; Quality Sport Images/Getty Images, p. 27.

Cover: Geert van Erven/Soccrates/Getty Images.